T0157485

Common Sense for the Man Who Doesn't Have Any

Or 40 Years A Jerk and How to Avoid Being One

"A clumsy, comical and sometimes serious look at the way one average man handled life until he realized he *really needed* to get a handle on it."

C. J. DAVIDSON

authorHOUSE®

AuthorHouse™
1663 Liberty Drive
Bloomington, IN 47403
www.authorhouse.com
Phone: 1 (800) 839-8640

Published by AuthorHouse   11/05/2015

ISBN: 978-1-5049-5855-4 (sc)
ISBN: 978-1-5049-5854-7 (e)

Contents

Acknowledgements

I'm sure that this is the place to start by thanking the Lord for my wife of over 40 years. I am thankful that she has been a faithful guinea pig for all that I have put her through and continue to.

Oops! There I go breaking rule number one to never call your wife or any of your children names, especially some kind of animal!

She has put up with my childishness, stubbornness, anger, vacillating, joblessness, discouragement, and thoughtlessness, and for what I thought was thought*ful*ness that ended up being thought*less*ness, because I thought *wrongly*. Plainly speaking, she has endured with a real jerk of a husband, thus the subtitle of this book.

I want to thank "my three sons" (some of you may remember the TV series by the same name) who have made most of this book possible for being **boys**; infants, toddlers, adolescents, teenagers, and yes, now, grown young men with families of their own. They are still feeding me with ammo by reminding me of things that happened during those years we were under one roof as a family and even present day events, while I have been writing this book.

Thank you, sons, for your patience and understanding with me as I was somewhat of a confused father, and being disconnected with life and feelings at times. Also, thanks for seeing the humor in some of the events that we went through together that you can bet will be in this book.

There are other family members, friends, and pastors who have given me words of admonition, challenge and encouragement along the way. You know who you are. Thank you!

Truly, "all glory and honor and power belongs to the Lord for in Him we live and move and have our being." Through the good, the bad and the ugly God has been here with me molding me into the child of His Kingdom that He wants me to be. "For it is God Who works in me both to will and to do for His good pleasure." (Philippians 2: 13)

"Oh, that men would give thanks to the Lord for His goodness and for His wonderful works to the children of men!" (Psalm 107: 21)

Thank you Lord!

Introduction

All names have been changed or not given to protect the innocent and to show grace to the guilty.

Mom and Dad never told me! They worked, took us to church, liked to eat out, and spent money! That's all I knew!

I'm a "Baby-boomer" child. Born in 1953 with a WWII Army veteran for a father and a nurse with almost 5 ½ years of experience under her hat at my birth, for a mother. I was the newest member of the family and the last. I have one sibling, my brother who is 2 ½ years older.

My earliest memories are playing in the snow in the cold Colorado winters, watching Hopalong Cassidy on the old box black and white TV, sitting in the green recliner sick with chickenpox, and the Christmas I got my Roy Rogers Ranch complete with Trigger and Nellie Belle. Life was good, from my perspective anyway.

My brother and I had our good times, but they didn't all end up so good like the time we were playing Tarzan by swinging off the clothes line post and my brother landed with his back bent and broke it, his back. Or the time we were jumping off of the concrete incinerator into a pile of tree trimmings and I got impatient for my turn and pushed him off and broke his wrist. There was also the time that we were at some friend's house and I got pushed down while my brother was barreling down the side walk on a tricycle and hit me in the head, sending me to the hospital for stitches in my forehead.

Probably my brother's fondest memory of our "good old days" was the time that our family got a new refrigerator. That meant there was a big box to mess around with, and that we did. We stood it up and climbed on top of it right next to the hedge and fence that looked over the busy north/south street beside our house. I was being my goofy self and waving and hollering at cars as they drove by.

Unbeknownst to me, Bob (the name we'll call my brother, to show him some grace), was carefully and stealthily pulling out the staples that held the box top together. I looked at him smiling, because I was having a good time with my bro, and he was smiling back at me, because he knew he was going to have an even better time in a very short order.

Suddenly, I felt the seat, the box top, start going down. I looked over at Bob with my eyes wide open with this look of, "What's happening?" Then, as we were looking at each other, me with a big question mark on my face and Bob with the biggest smile on his, "Whoosh," down we went together through the box into the dark and to the ground. For Bob this was a CreditCard moment, priceless.

One of the things that mom and dad never told me was about girls and "the birds and the bees." I don't remember ever hearing that story! I liked girls. I just didn't know anything about them.

Not until I was a married adult and struggling with a family of my own, did I realize that I was never told *a lot of things* that I needed to hear from my parents or from some other informed adult. It did not dawn on me until I was in my 40's that I am a product of a broken home. Both of my parents came from homes where their parents divorced and at one point a parent just left the family with multiple children in the house. No wonder I hadn't been told some things. They had never heard them either!

I am not putting the blame on my parents for the way I turned out with all of my issues and vices. This is what one of my favorite preacher/authors has written about in his book No More Excuses. We can try and play "the blame game," but that's all it is, a game, an excuse for not taking personal responsibility to do the hard work it takes to make positive changes in our lives. As King Solomon wrote in Ecclesiastes 3: 1, "For everything there is a season, and a time for every purpose under heaven," and it's time that we get a handle on our lives and keep a grip on them. Keep learning. Keep growing. Keep saying "I'm sorry!" Keep saying "I love you," and "I forgive you!" And remember that your family and friends and church, your *world* is important. People are important! Life isn't really all about me, about you. It's about us!!

What is in this book is shared from a married man's perspective, but young and old, single and separated alike can learn from it. We all need to think right. We all need to talk right. We all need to grow up and find that balance in our lives that makes us strong, wise, compassionate, and useful in our community and world.

As I wrote on the title page, this is "a clumsy, comical, and sometimes serious look at the way an average man handled life until he realized he *really needed* to get a handle on it!" So, what are you waiting for? Hang on for the ride!

Chapter 1

Bricks and Gentlemen

Bricks

The first thing that I need to do is to define these terms, names.

-a brick-"a handy-sized building material typically being rectangular and about 2 ¼ x 3 ¾ x 8 inches and of moist clay hardened by heat, a rectangular compressed mass; a gaffe, blunder; an unintelligent person, "dumb as a brick." From Webster's & Urban dictionaries.

Syn.- a rock. a blockhead, an airhead, a hot head, a screw ball, a jerk, etc., etc.

Now, of course, I'm not calling every man unintelligent or stupid. But, a lot of us can be just downright bricks! Am I right? How many of you have embarrassed your wife or your children in public? Please, don't do it!

I remember being with my wife at a harvest time costume banquet (that's what you call it when you are at a church or Christian camp at Halloween time) and I was dressed like a lumber jack. There must have been 25 or 30 people there and we were asked to go around the room and introduce ourselves. So, my mind started whirling about who we could be, some familiar couple. Then it hit me!

When it came our turn I said, "I'm Paul Bunyan and this is my wife Babe." Now she was wearing a beautiful medium blue dress and was quite pregnant with our third son. I am almost positive that I *did not* add at the end of "Babe," "the Blue Ox!" She says I did, but even that long ago I was wise enough not to do that to her. Still, even if I didn't call her an ox everyone there knew who Babe was. I really should not have gone there. Of course, I got the eye and the word about *that* one. But, did I learn from that event? Nope!

I guess I had run-off-at-the-mouth a few times because we were at another group function, a church one, no less, and I did it again. We were once more asked to introduce ourselves, and this time my wife leaned over to me and said not to say something "off-the-cuff" that would be embarrassing. *It wasn't even on my mind*! Until then!

Once again, it was our turn and I said, "I'm Buford Northington, the Third and this is my wife Bertha." *Whoa*! What was I thinking? I wasn't! By this time she was the mother of three sons and if you are a married man and have children you know what can happen to a woman in that scenario.

And I really don't remember the shape of her figure at that time or even really noticed, because I loved her just the way she was. She was my wife, *for crying out loud,* and the mother of our three handsome sons. She was very embarrassed, not only because she may have been feeling some way about herself, but that I had called her *Bertha*. There was some other familiar fictional character around at that same time period named "Bertha Butt." Wow! Had I done it this time!!

By the way, if you have the tendency to speak "off-the-cuff," think first! If you have something on your cuff it's probably something you don't want on it, that's not supposed to be there. So, take care of it!

One final, real example of what a brick looks and acts like.

For those of you who are married and you appreciate neatness and organization, be sure that you don't complain about your wife's housekeeping. If it is not as nice as you would like it, be willing to help with it!

When we were first married my wife was one of those little-Susie-homemaker types and I was very glad. This was a great step upward from college dorm life with guys who either did not care about neatness and cleanliness or were just afraid to get their hands dirty. Most of the ones I roomed with would not even take their turn to clean the commode. It got pretty gross.

By the time we had three little guys of our own running around the house the neatness fact was beginning to change. I would be gone all day working while my wife was home trying to keep up with three, five and seven year olds, doing laundry, cooking, house cleaning, and whatever else a young mother had to do to keep a home going.

So, what did I do one day? When I got home from work I stepped through the door and saw some socks and toys on the floor and said something like, "This house is a mess!"

You can bet how *that* went over! I was spoiled, spoiled from the "honeymoon" before children came along. Instead of complaining about a few clothes and toys lying around, I needed to pitch in and help. I wasn't thinking. Instead I was opening my big mouth and inserting foot, size 10 ½D.

As my wife has told me many times, even lately, "Never pass up an opportunity to keep your mouth shut!" Great advice!

Men! Don't be bricks, jerks! Enough said.

Gentlemen

It's time to talk about what it means to be a gentleman.
-a gentleman-"a man whose conduct conforms to a high standard of propriety or correct behavior. A man of any social class or condition-often used in a courteous reference." Webster's dictionary

A gentleman is a guy who believes in manners, courtesies, etc., etc.

First of all, let's consider old-fashioned manners. What's wrong with them? Everything old-fashioned is not necessarily out of date. We still sit in chairs don't we? We still wear shoes, right? Some of you are living in houses that are 50, 60, 70 years old! I would call that old-fashioned. And some of you may even own and are driving a car that is over 20 years old.

In case you didn't know it, a car 20 years old is considered an antique and you can buy an antique plate for it and never have to pay another tag fee! My town car is a 1968 VW Beetle, which is better known as a "Bug." There's nothing like driving around town in a vintage Bug that gets people smiling. It happens every time I drive it. Now, I'm sure that they are either thinking about the good old days when they owned one or that they just like how cute it looks. They're surely not *laughing* at me for still driving around in such an old-fashioned car!

Speaking of chairs. Yes, I mentioned chairs! It is still okay for you to pull out the chair at the table to help a lady sit down, and to open the door to your old house or your 20 year old car for her. These are manners, courtesies, chivalrous things that you can do to show that you have some gentlemanly qualities.

Really, brains can get you a lot further than brawn. It doesn't hurt to have *some* muscle. You do have to have them to pull out chairs and open doors!

One more thing about table manners. Oh yeah, we haven't even talked about those! There was one thing about table manners that I had to learn when we moved to "The South." When you have guests in your home for a meal or if you are the guest in someone else's abode, you should not dig into your grub as soon as the plate is set in front of your face. You are to wait until everyone is served and the hostess is seated and takes her first bite of food. *Then*, you can stuff your pie hole, being careful not to splatter any food particles on those sitting near you.

Now when it comes to dessert, the rule, lately, is that the hostess tells you to go ahead and eat it before it gets cold or melts, which ever the case may be. I guess there is something extra special about desserts than that of the main course. I don't understand it all. I just try to remember and obey the rules.

In our modern, technologically advanced, socially aware, freedom seeking society, there are some women who think that they don't want men to be gentlemen nor enjoy chivalry.

Ladies

We should probably take a moment here and define *a lady*;
-**a lady**-a woman of refinement and gentle manners-often used in a courteous reference, the wife of a knight, baronet, member of the peerage, or one having the courtesy title of *lord* and used as a courtesy title for the daughter of a duke. Webster's dictionary.

I would venture to say that most of us don't fall into the last part of that definition, a knight or lord. It may be that these women don't want to be ladies, "women of refinement, with gentle manners and courteous!" So, don't fight it! But, also don't let these non-ladies cause you to forget that the rest of the world of women appreciate and need a gentleman and his considerate ways.

Also, part of being a gentleman is being careful what comes out of your mouth during moments of frustration. Don't be a potty mouth!

When I was growing up we were not allowed to use the "*f*" or "*s*" words. Not <u>those</u> two words! Of course not! I mean the other f and s words, fart and shut up. There is another word that my wife and I did not allow in our home with our boys, the "*c*" word. You know, *crap*! Unfortunately, that word flew freely from my father at our house in my formative years and I didn't even know what it meant except that he was upset when he used it.

When I got married the *c* word was added to the list of those verbal exclamations that were "no-nos." First of all, potty language is bathroom talk, as I was told, and it *belonged* in the bathroom with those actual bodily functions, if said at all! More on that subject later.

My wife grew up in a Christian home and, in her home the "*s*" word, shut-up, was never used. If it did get used at all it was saved for dogs and the devil. Yes! You could tell a dog that was yapping its fool head off to, "Shut up!" And, if the devil was trying to tell you to do something that you knew mom and dad told you not to do and that you were pretty sure the Bible was against, you could say just what Jesus said, "Shut up Satan, and get thee behind Me!"

Now I'll have to admit, since our boys are grown and gone, these words have seemed to slip out of my mouth more than I care to say, especially the *c* word. And I blame that on my upbringing *and* my oldest son. As I said, the *c* word, was used liberally when I was young. But then, for some reason while our oldest son was still living with us in his early 20's and attending college, and waiting to go into the military, *he* started using it! Why? I don't know! So, I guess I figured since our boys were all grown up now and decided they could use this word and the others, it was okay for me to use them too!

But, really guys, I mean, gentlemen, we need to watch our mouths and mind our manners around the ladies *and* the women and children too.

Chapter 2

Burps, Sneezes and Other Bodily Functions

Now you may be wondering why this was not part of having good manners. Well, because there is no way of making *any part* of these good manners in public, and most of them are hard to avoid. They are not usually something you do, they are something that is done *to* you!

Maybe I should have titled this chapter, "Burps, Sneezes, and Other Bodily Functions That You Are Not Sure How They Are Caused and Wish You Could Eliminate." I don't know of anyone that enjoys having these things come up so suddenly, interrupting their lives and embarrassing and inconveniencing them. Well, I can think of maybe one of these functions that *some* people do, and get a laugh out of it. I'm sure you know what I mean and know who you are.

Burps

-**burping** (also known as belching, ructus, or eructation) is the release of gas from the digestive tract (mainly esophagus and stomach) through the mouth. It is usually accompanied with a typical sound and, at times, an odor. Wikipedia.

I have never even heard of two of those terms! And the definition doesn't say anything about what causes them, just gas! And where did the gas come from? Maybe I should have looked it up in Webster's instead of wikipedia. Hey! I was already sitting at the computer. I would have had to get up and take two steps behind me and reach for the dictionary!

Most of the time a burp comes unexpectedly, so what can you do about it? If I could ever figure out exactly what causes them, I would certainly do what I could to not burp. Although, I have had many that were pleasant reminders of some food that I had eaten recently. As I have been known to say, when I suppose I wasn't thinking, not being wise, "That tasted as good second time around!" Sometimes it has tasted even *better*!

If you have the misfortune of having a belching attack in public, the polite thing to do is apologize profusely, turn red and continue on with whatever you were doing before you were so rudely interrupted. That's about it!

Now, if you are by yourself, that's another thing. Most burps are "accompanied with a typical sound." Who says they all have to be *typical*? You can have what I call a time of *private creativity*. I think that my father-in-law kind of taught me this. But, I have expanded on it, in private, for the most part.

What do I mean? Well, when you do have some burps that you feel coming on, make the most of them! Bring them up with some flare, creativity, a *sensible* sound. Yell it! Bark! Growl! Whatever! If you have to burp, be creative, when in *private*.

I have even heard people speak a line and sing their burps. These are the people who want a laugh and need the attention.

There is one hazard about belching that my boys call a *vurp*. What's a vurp?

Vurps

-a **vurp**-is a burp that brings up with it some previously chewed and swallowed food. In other words, a little vomit comes up in your mouth, thus, the word vurp. A fancier way of saying it comes from the Slang dictionary; "When a little bit of the stomach contents (usually bile) is expelled into the esophagus, also known as wet burps."

Now, you can probably avoid having vurps if you don't eat too much at mealtime and/or don't do some hard physical labor soon after eating. A word to the wise.

Sneezes

-**a sneeze**, or sternutation, is a semi-autonomous, convulsive expulsion of air from the lungs through the nose and mouth, usually caused by foreign particles irritating the nasal mucosa. A sneeze expels air forcibly from the mouth and nose in an explosive, spasmodic involuntary action resulting chiefly from irritation of the nasal membrane. Wikipedia

How's that for a definition?! Sounds like an attorney wrote it. Maybe dictionaries are where they get their lawyering language from. Well, of course!

As I have been saying, here is another one of those bodily functions that comes on as a "spasmodic involuntary action," or very unexpectedly. Better carry a tissue or two!

If you have troubles with allergies you know all about this one. They can make you more miserable when you are going through a spell or have a cold. And what a mess they can make of your face and anybody else's that may be in the path of your sneeze when the mucus is bountiful! We can all say, "Yuck!"

Here, again is a function that you can be creative with, in private, *if* you feel them coming. Sneeze a loud "Achoo!" Drag it out! Play with it! Need to be careful here too. You can over do it and really hurt yourself.

I have to be very, very careful with creative sneezes these days. I have a condition called, believe it or not*, costochondritis.* Really! Okay, I might as well give you this definition as well.

Costochondritis

-**costochondritis**-the inflammation of the costal cartilages, that is characterized by pain of the anterior chest wall that may radiate. The American Heritage Medical Dictionary.

In layman's terms, it is the pulling away of the cartilage from around the ribs caused by some kind of strenuous action. Mine is in the right ribs and boy can it be painful and radiate when I sneeze. I have the habit now of holding my ribs before I sneeze. But, if one comes on before I know it or if I have my hands full and can't hold on, "Yeow! Where did the guy go that just stabbed me in the ribs?!" It is most commonly known as a golfer's injury. I guess swinging all those boxes around through the years working in shipping and receiving can do the same thing to you as swinging a golf club. Who knew?

So, you see, sneezing can have its perils. If there is one thing that plenty of pockets in your pants and shirts are good for, it's for plenty if tissues. Always go out in public prepared.

Hiccups

Now here's an annoying malady! I think they are part of an evil spell! But, the dictionary says otherwise.

-**hiccups**-involuntary contractions of the diaphragm. Each contraction is followed by a sudden closure of the vocal cords, which produces the characteristic "hic" sound. Hiccups may result from a large meal, alcoholic beverages or sudden excitement. Mayo Clinic website.

So, be careful how much you eat, what you drink and how much fun you have. I've gotten hiccups without doing *any* of those things, I think!

When they last for what seems like an eternity, you start remembering some of those remedies. You can blow in a paper bag until your face turns blue or until you pass out. That definitely stops them. Kind of stops your whole body, except your breathing. If that doesn't work you can drink some water. If that doesn't work you can drink some more water. And, then if it still hasn't cured them, at least you have gotten your necessary amount of water for the day. You may not be hungry for the next meal, either, 'cause you're bloated!

Oh, yeah! There's the simple hold-your-breath method too! Works every time, doesn't it? You sit there with your cheeks bulging out like a hamster with his cheeks stuffed with, whatever! Then your eyes start to bug out and you feel like you can't hold it any longer! So, you let it all out. You're cured! Nope. They're still there. Rats!!

You can even have somebody try to scare you to get rid of them. I thought that was one of the things that *caused* them, "sudden excitement!"

After trying all of the myths and folklore to rid yourself of this unexpected, involuntary annoyance, you go on with whatever you need to do and notice, *they're gone*! Yea!! But what worked to make them stop? Oh well.

I just have one further word on this topic of bodily functions. This is for *adults only*! Okay, if you are 16 and older, read on.

If hiccups are part of an evil spell, then this next bodily function is the whole enchilada!

Flatulence

-**flatulence**-is gas in the intestines that is expelled from the anus which originates from the normal breakdown of undigested foods by bacteria that normally live in the colon. On average, people have gas 14 times a day. Symptomfind.com

This is the one bodily function that most decent people don't want to talk about or want to say is a problem if they even would admit it exists. I guess that I'm not a decent person then, because I'm writing about it.

Flatulence, passing gas or as the boys from the children's home taught us when our family moved in with them, *pooting* (from the booty), or as seems to be the most common term used today, you know, the farting word. It happens to most people, on average, 14 times a day.

Fourteen times a day! That almost makes me want to consciously start counting. And all the foods that can produce the stuff makes it awful hard to avoid having it: breads, potatoes, beans, cheese, other milk products, onions, carbonated drinks, etc., etc., etc. Talk about this being the whole enchilada. The ingredients are all there!

Since this seems to be so hard to avoid, let me make this one suggestion. When you are out in public, at someone else's home or at church with the family, never be afraid to let your child slip out for a moment if there is the chance of an explosion of the intestinal kind. Better the slight distraction by leaving the room than the embarrassment and interruption of the whole event! There is one very recent personal story that I could share on this subject, but, I think I had better *pass* on that. Get it?

To go along with this subject, there is something that has developed in more recent years that use to be considered just a female infliction. It's called IBS, Irritable Bowel Syndrome. It's not just for woman anymore. I know, because I have it and I like to call it *Impromptu Bowel Surges*, because you never know what's coming, or not, and when!

And here's the common sense to go with this one. Watch your diet! No, you don't need to go *on* a diet, well, maybe some of you should if you are 30 pounds or more over weight. Be careful what and how much you eat, drink plenty of fluids, mostly water, and take a daily enzyme, probiotic supplement. Now I'm no doctor or nutritionist, but having put up with this for 10 years, reading and listening and experimenting on myself, I have found that a little dietary discipline makes a *world* of difference.

I think this pretty much covers the subject. Moving right along…

Chapter 3

Dirty Socks and TP Holders

"You wore them and got them dirty, so you put them away!
They don't belong on the floor.
No! Don't put them *back* in your dresser!
I *know* that's where you got them!
They're dirty now! *Put them in the dirty clothes hamper!!*"

Does this sound familiar? It's not just socks! Shoes, shirts, pants, and of course, the tidy whiteys, or whichever kind of undies you wear, should not be all over your floor and room. "There is a place for everything and everything in its place!"

When I was growing up with an older brother this was certainly an issue. By the time we were in our early teens we had separate rooms. In my brother's room was an old upholstered double seat from a railroad passenger car. He started using it as the place to pile up his clothes after wearing them each day. You never wore the same thing *two days in a row* when you were in junior high school!

The only problem with this technique was that clothes did not get into the hamper and get laundered on a regular basis. So, when he wanted to wear a particular item, he would dig through the pile on the chair, shake it out, sniff it, and, if it passed the sniff test, threw it into the dryer to get out the wrinkles. There! Good as.., well, good enough.

I didn't have a big chair in my room, but I *did* have a four poster bed. So, guess what I used the posters for? Clothes hangers!! My routine and technique was pretty much the same as my brother's; unbury what I wanted to wear, sniff it, and maybe, throw it into the dryer. There was one advantage to the bedpost; the shirts were all draped over each other instead of piled on top, so wrinkling was not as bad.

You may be asking yourself by now, "What were you doing putting half dirty clothes on your *clean* body?!" Who said anything about a *clean* body? We are talking about learning some common sense here. And this is another example of the lack thereof. We were brought up with the philosophy that "you took a bath on Saturday night whether you needed it or not." Need I say more? I know, gross, huh?

Clothes hampers, clothes hangers and clothes closets are all great inventions and each has a single purpose. I hope that this is not any of you these days! This was more aimed at your children that you as mature men should be helping teach them to do and *not* to do.

Don't make me have to draw you a picture! I'm no Picasso! (I just looked up the ten most popular Picassos. I think I could actually do as well as some of those! Maybe I should take up charcoal drawing after I finish this book! Hmm)!

If this did hit home with some of you, you've got a real problem! Did you even read chapter one? Do you need to read it again? This problem would put you in the class of "a brick", leaning more towards a real lazy, thoughtless *jerk*! Your wives are not your mothers, nannies or nurses that personally clean you, feed you, change you, or pick up after you! I hope that hurts, uh, helps!

Neatness, guys! Organization! And, more importantly, consideration for your wife! That is the first letter in the word *Love*! Yes, true love is spelled c-a-r-e:

C-consideration

A-appreciation

R-respect

E-effort, edification

Consideration

-**consideration**-thinking about the other person's needs and desires, "continuous careful thought," deliberate attention to matters, "sympathetic regard or notice." Merriam-Webster Dictionary.

In other words, open your eyes! Turn on your brain! Look around and do the little things. Be considerate!

Speaking of little things, I feel sorry for the guy who doesn't even know how to take the empty toilet paper roll off the tp holder and put on a new one. Don't keep frustrating your wife when she goes to use the bathroom and at the inappropriate time to, once again, find that "*There's no toilet paper on the holder!*" Come on guys!!

This was an issue back in college. One of my roommates would not lift a finger, not even to get out more toilet paper when he used the last of it. I asked him one day, "Why won't you do anything around here?" His answer? "Mother did all of that (for me)." It was right after this that he stopped using the dorm apartment bathroom all together and just went to the college gym locker-room to shower, etc. I don't know how he even got his clothes washed. He must have sent them home to mommy every weekend. The poor gal that ever fell in love with *that* man.

Appreciation

-**appreciation**-"the *recognition and enjoyment* of the *good qualities* of *someone* or something. Syns-*valuing, treasuring,* admiration. OxfordDictionaries. (emphasis mine)

The definition pretty much says it all. Men, recognize and enjoy the good qualities of the special lady in your life. Tell her what a great job she is doing.

I imagine that most of you men who are married have wives who work outside the home. (I wish there was more of a trend for wives and mothers being able and willing to be at home. It would be better for all of us. Go ahead, call me a male chauvinist, if you must). If your wife does have a job that requires her to work somewhere in the workforce, it is doubly important that you make her feel considered and appreciated. It's not easy to have a career, a husband, children, and a house to care for. Do what you can to make her feel special.

No brag, just fact! This is the list of things that get done at our house every week by you know who, *me*;

-make beds

-empty trash

-do the laundry

-vacuum, sweep and mop floors

-a little dusting (something I don't do well enough)

-vehicle maintenance (mostly with the help of professionals these days)

-clean sinks

-cook supper a couple times a week (something new for me in the last year and a half)

And, yes..,

-scrub commodes!

Do both the little and the big things that she can't or shouldn't need to worry about.

Respect

-**respect**-to admire someone or something deeply, as a result of their abilities, qualities and achievements. Oxford Dictionaries.

This sounds a lot like appreciation. Respect goes hand-in-hand with it. To respect your wife is to truly enjoy her for the person she is, for the abilities she possesses, not just because of what she can give you to meet *your* every need. See her as a person who has needs, too. Do what you can to meet them.

One of those big things you can do for her is *listen!* Listen means…

L-learn

I-information

S-so

T-things

E-end up

N-nicely

You have to listen, really listen to get the information that she is trying to communicate! And listening has to be without you talking while she is talking!! Let her words resonate and filter through all the other stuff going on in your head. Assimilate! Take in *all* the words and information she is giving you, so you can try to fully understand what she needs from you! Listen, learn and then act on what you have heard and learned.

15

I have this thing about thinking of something and then speaking about it from the end of the thought. It can frustrate my wife. Let me illustrate.

Me- "That's pretty funny! (just speaking "out of the blue")
My wife-"What's funny? What did you say? Did I miss something?"
Me-"I was just thinking about the doctor telling me that all my blood work looked good and that I was as healthy as a horse, and thinking then, why do I feel as weak as a kitten?"
My wife-"You have told me to be honest with you and honestly, it frustrates me for you to start a conversation in the middle or end of your thought. It makes me feel like I have not been listening or that I should know what you are talking about!
Would you please not do that?"

I hope that I have gotten the point now! I have my excuses for forgetting this one in the past. First, in the beginning of our relationship it was due to simple immaturity. I did not know any better. Then, after several years of marriage, I must have done it out of familiarity, habit, or being oblivious to how it made her feel. But, now, after nearly 41 years together, it *has* to be senility. Really! I am having a harder time than I have ever had thinking, thinking correctly, and remembering.

Back to how to spell love.

Love is consideration, appreciation, respect, and, wait for it, good *old-fashioned* effort!

Effort

-**effort**-a vigorous or determined attempt. Oxford Dictionaries.

And, to go along with that…,

-**edification**-instruction or improvement of a person morally and intellectually; guidance. Oxford Dictionaries.

Love *is* caring, and both of these words are action words. Love is more than feelings and words. Love, love that lasts, takes effort. Part of that effort is edifying her, building her up by encouraging her by *you* being the man that she needs you to be. Have you heard this song by Chris Young written by Tim Nichols and Brett James?

I wanna be a good man
A 'do like I should' man
I wanna be the kind of man the mirror likes to see
I wanna be a strong man
And admit that I was wrong man
God I'm asking you to come change me
To the man I wanna be

If you ever come home some evening and find your wife crying her eyes out, it may be that her "love tank" is running on empty. Fill it up with gallons of c-a-r-e. Gentlemen, think! Listen! Care for your family!

You can start by picking up those dirty socks on the floor!

Chapter 4

Bedtime Stories and Messy Diapers

I am so thankful for books and the ability to read. This was not always the case. Reading has always been difficult for me. When I was supposed to be learning to read, I wanted to play, talk and clown around. If there had been the diagnoses ADD or ADHD back in the 1960's I would probably have been labeled one who had it.

As far as I was concerned, school was just a place to be around more kids my age who enjoyed the same things that I did; running through the playground yelling my head off, playing kick ball and marbles, and chasing the girls and trying to kiss them. It was the same at home. All I wanted to do was play with my toys and with the neighbor kids.

Apparently, my teacher told my parents that I was having trouble with my reading skills (and I'm sure she told them a lot more about some of my other skills), because I can remember on one occasion having to sit between my parents on the couch in the living room and they wanting me to read to them.

Well, it didn't work! If my memory serves me well (it seems to work okay for all of my ancient life history, but not for what happened just five minutes ago. What did happen five minutes ago?) I made such a fuss and cried and carried on that my parents just gave up on me and let me have my foolish way. I was pretty much on my own from then on when it came to school.

I bluffed my way through the next 10 years of academia with the help of a school system that was basically giving out "social promotions" to a large number of students. If you are not familiar with that term, it simply means that as long as a student didn't beat up a teacher in class or a fellow student and was in class the required amount of days per year, he was promoted to the next grade all the way to graduation, so no teacher had to look at him for more than one year. It did not seem to matter what a kid knew or didn't know, just file them through to graduation and then let *society* worry about them.

The bluffing stopped my senior year when my English teacher required us to read two books of at least 110 pages and give reports on them. That's when I learned about "Classics Illustrated" comic books! These are comic size and form *with pictures* of the classics like "Moby Dick, Ivanhoe, and Treasure Island." Wow! That was great! I bought "The Man Without a Country," read it and gave my report. Cool! At least I thought it was cool then. But, my girlfriend at the time, thought otherwise. I ended up confessing to my teacher what I had done and she let me slide on one condition. She would give me credit for the comic book only if I read a book of 110 pages for the second report. So, I did read over 110 pages of a Reader's Digest Condensed version of "The Green Helmet". It still was not a complete book, but *it was 110 pages*!! A milestone for me!

I am so thankful for that girlfriend who had the boldness to tell me that I was wrong. This somewhat prepared me for the next big step in my life, five years of Bible college.

If a person could go back in time and change the way they did things, one of the things I would try and do differently is learn to read well and find the joy and self confidence in doing so.

Having said all of this, I'm glad I can read, fairly well, and that because I learned the importance of it, I read to my boys when they were young. I wanted them to learn to love reading. I am so thankful that most of the time while they were growing up I was home from work before their bedtime. Bedtime was story time for daddy and his sons. Sometimes, it was also wrestle and tickle time before reading. (That usually came earlier in the evening, because that physical stuff could make it hard for them to be settled down for reading and lights out. We didn't need them to be over-stimulated).

Stories at bedtime were daddy time with the boys. Good times with good books. This also meant some mommy time for herself. This was good for everybody.

Men, don't be too busy to read to your children and to listen to them tell you about their day! Read! Read! Read to your children! They need it! You may not be the best reader yourself or even like to read that much, but don't let them know it! This is one of the best gifts you can give to your family, a love for reading! It is a much better source of entertainment than TV, video games and now, texting, tweeting, and whatever all the rest of that handheld stuff is called. A person can go anywhere in the *world* and learn about anything they need and want to know by *reading*. I hope that learning aspect includes this little volume. I am letting you into my world and sharing lessons and experiences that could possibly be helpful to you.

Along with spending time reading to your children, which can give your wife a much needed break, so she can try and super glue some hair back on her head that she may have pulled out, or whatever she may need to put back together, there is the sharing of another blessing, *messy diapers*! Who says the wife has to change them all?! You helped bring those little poop factories into the world! Unless you have an uncontrollable gag reflex or are allergic to bodily fluids *and* solids, you need to take your turn changing diapers. Man up!!

Maybe I'm special. I don't mean *that* kind of special, though some people may think I'm a certain kind of special, a special *case*, quirky. Anyway, I may be different. Now that is undeniable by most! What I'm trying to say is that I had the opportunity to change my first diaper when I was in the 6th or 7th grade. That may not sound young to some, because I am sure that there are a lot of girls who changed kids diapers at an earlier age than that. But, for the most part, guys didn't do that kind of thing at 11 or 12 years old! I remember volunteering to babysit a family's sick youngest son, so that they could go to church on Sunday morning. The father was the song leader and his wife played the piano. I felt like "big stuff" to be trusted to care for this one year old at their house, and best of all, to miss going to church!!

Not much longer after the rest of the family was gone, *it* came! I was probably told that I would need to check his diaper, but I wasn't expecting *this*! I must have smelled something, so I did give a look and sure enough

I *found*! Fortunately, what I found was done and in one piece. No biggie! Dropped it, wiped it, and slapped on a clean one. This was back in the 60's before, I think, disposables were even invented. So, it was the cloth diaper and the plastic pants over it. I felt pretty proud of myself and didn't even think about throwing up!

We used cloth diapers in our family into the mid 80's. But, I do remember on one trip from California to Colorado with two in diapers, that we splurged and bought some disposables. Now, when you are driving all day across CA, AZ, to your final destination in 1978 with no rest areas and one of the boys has a blow out, what do you do? Well, you pull over to the side of the road in the middle of the desert, make the change, and, since you don't want that smelly thing in the car with you for another 5 hours, you place it under one of the *millions* of rocks lying on either side of the highway. That's what you do! I felt bad about that for a moment, but then thought, "Who's goin' know?!" And, if some guy does come along and lifts up *that* rock, he's got to have the *dumbest* luck in the world!

So, not to drag this out much further, let me say this. Men, just because you are all grown up and know how to "put *your* poop in the potty" (a new phrase that grandma and grandpa have learned in the last 4 years or so), doesn't mean you are exempt from diaper duty. Besides, someone had to do this for you when you were a little *pooper*! (Am I writing too much about bodily functions? This *is* a book for guys!) If you live long enough you may have to depend on your children to change *your* Depends! You might want to remind them from time to time about all those messy diapers of theirs that you changed.

How's this for a good bedtime story?

Chapter 5

Utility bills, Hand Soap, and Thermostats

Everything costs so much these days. Unless you are rich, money is *the* precious commodity today and we all need to be careful how we spend it and find ways to save it.

I tried to do my part to "save the world" and make a little money by doing some recycling. Where we live now there is no place that buys it all, so I stopped collecting them because of the time it took. Besides, I figured that the little bit I was recycling was not even a drop in the bucket to what is dumped into the county landfill on a daily basis. There is a recycling program in our town, but the City is in on it and wants to charge me $4 a month for *me* to help *them* make more money on what they pick up off my curb!

Now that I've got that off my chest! I have other ways to spend my time. This earth is not going to last forever! It's all going to be burned up and renovated, hopefully, someday soon! Until that great day comes, there are some things that you can do to keep a few more bucks in your pocket between paychecks.

If you have older children in your household here are some tips on saving on utility bills. Once you have taught your kids the importance of personal hygiene, it seems that when they become tweens to teens there is the mindset of overdoing it in this area. Showers, shampoo, soap, toilet paper, and toothpaste all tend to disappear like a paycheck due to taxes.

We have one boy who took the longest and hottest showers he could *everyday*! I told him on many occasions that he needed to take shorter ones. Ten minutes is long enough for a shower. If you can't get clean in 10 minutes you've got a problem! Well, he did have a problem and it was becoming *my* problem! I even set a timer and put it in the bathroom so he would hear it and know when "time is up!"

That didn't work either. But, I'll tell you what did. I warned him if his water was not off by the time the beeping started on the timer that he was going to be taking "a cold shower" in the middle of winter. He either forgot what I had told him or didn't believe that I could be so cruel.

The next morning when he got into the shower I set the timer and it went off after 10 minutes. Wouldn't you know it! His shower kept *going*. He made me have to keep my word and go outside under the carport and turn off the hot water heater. When I got back into the house I heard him hollering something like, "AAAAAAA! OHHH! The water's freezing cold!" We never had another problem with long showers by *any* of the boys after that. (I wouldn't recommend that technique on anyone with heart trouble.) It did seem that a bar of soap and a bottle of shampoo lasted a lot longer.

Then, there's the toilet paper and toothpaste. In both cases a "little dab 'ill do ya!" Nowadays, it doesn't take half a roll of tp to get the job done. Thank goodness for the invention of wet wipes! (Here I go again! Maybe I should have covered this in chapter 3).

If you have a problem with your plumbing as we did, you certainly don't want too much paper going down the commode and causing *more* trouble. Of course, it isn't only the paper that can be the issue. The lack of fiber in one's diet can be part of it, or most of it. Fresh fruits and veggies in your daily diet work wonders! Catch my drift? Once again, don't make me have to draw you a picture, although, I did once draw a picture in grade school of things that you can *smell* in a little book that we had to make about "Our Five Senses."

Toothpaste is another wonderful personal hygiene invention. But, how much of the stuff does it take to get your teeth clean? Not much, really. It's all in the time and technique of brushing that produces the real cleaning. When you are brushing your teeth and you see yourself in the mirror and you look like a rabid animal, you're using too much paste. You are supposed to be cleaning your teeth, not your whole face! I can make a tube last for six months! Can you?

Another way to save money on utilities deals with laundry. Unless you or one of your children has that affliction of excessive perspiration or hyperhidrosis, clothes are not necessarily dirty after one wear, especially in the winter. I guess, depending on your work and other activities, it may be that you need clean shirts and pants every day. But, if you just sit around in a classroom or office eight hours a day, when you get home take them off, give them "the sniff test", and hang them up for another day. I'm not saying that you don't need to change your socks and undies every day! For other tips on how to care for your clothes, refer back to chapter 3.

One of the best ways to keep more money in the checkbook is to master the use of the thermostat. When I say master, I mean *you* be the master controller of the thermostat "winter, spring, summer, or fall. It doesn't matter at all," because you'll be there. You've got a friend, your central air unit.

You could have a family meeting and discuss this issue and hopefully agree on suitable temperature settings for all seasons. Fat chance of that happening! I have discovered that every person in the family seems to have a different physical internal thermostat, so there is usually never an agreement on this. You, the master, decide on a reasonable temperature range, set the thermostat, and either pass out the sweaters and gloves or have them strip to their tees and skivvies, depending on what time of year it is.

Don't *even* get me started on "programmable thermostats!" Those things are for people who have a worse memory than mine! Or, for those who are single individuals who don't have multiple internal thermostats to contend with. Besides, you about have to be an IT person to know how to set the stupid things! I need to use my brain power for more important functions on a daily basis. I can push the little up and down arrows on mine just fine!

What I am doing right now is turning down the thermostat to 68 during the day and huddling up in my man cave, the study, with a small tower heater. I hope this saves a few dollars a month.

Most houses do have windows and some have ceiling fans. Weather and humidity permitting, windows opened to create a cross breeze work well for no-cost cooling in early spring and late summer to early fall. Just be sure you have screens on the windows. Did I need to add that? There it is, just in case.

Ceiling fans are great and cheaper than running the central air. Here is a little tip about fans. If you are not going to be in a room for some time or are going to leave the house for awhile, turn them off. They only move the air and create evaporation to make you *feel* cooler while you are near them. They don't actually lower the temp in a room. This is somewhat of a debate in our house. I have finally given in and let the fans run in a room or two even when nobody is occupying them for an hour or so. But, after that much time, "click," off they go!

The final item that can help on the utility costs is telephone usage. The only thing that used to be a real problem with phones was making too many long distance calls. We were very strict and frugal with the long distance conversations. Now you can get unlimited long distance if you get the deluxe plan with call forwarding, voice messaging, texting, and all the rest for 100 bucks a month *or* more. Not every member of the family <u>needs</u> a phone! If they think otherwise, have them get a job and pay for it themselves. I think it would be cheaper to go back about 20 years and just pay for the long distance.

About texting while walking, talking, driving, which most tragically has caused too many deaths, let's not do it except when we are sitting still and not doing anything else. Isn't that the common sense thing to do?!

Chapter 6

Fireworks, Doggy Doo and Carpet Stains

What is it with us guys and fire?! We like bonfires, campfires, fireplaces, houses and buildings on fire, and fireworks. Yeah! It's just a guy thing for the most part, a fascination with fire! I don't think women are too much into it. They have their own fascinations and obsessions.

Fire was created by God. He must have introduced it to Adam and Eve in the Garden of Eden, because they needed something to wear after they messed up big time.

> And the LORD God made clothing from animal skins for Adam and his wife. (Genesis 3: 21).

Nothing was wasted. God used fire to burn the necessary sacrifice in the presence of Adam and Eve. The very first BBQ prepared by the Lord Himself.

I just finished reading I Kings 18 about Elijah and the fire contest on Mount Carmel. That had to be quite a sight. *Fire* from heaven! No sticks rubbed together. No oil and torch. Just Almighty God sending down fire from the sky in the dark of night! It burned up the wood and the stone altar and the water that had been poured all over it! Truly *awesome*!

My brother and I liked fire as kids. There was this one time that we decided to start one in the backyard, a nice yard with lawn extending about three quarters of the way back. Why the last quarter was just dirt, I don't know. Maybe our dad was thinking he might plant a garden or something. I don't know. It was a good thing that there was *just* dirt. That's where we started a small fire. No sooner was it burning good, than dad came barreling out the door! How did he know we were "playing with fire?!" We thought he was sleeping! I think he was, but the phone woke him up. A neighbor, Mrs. Parker, from the house cattie-corner behind ours called. Dear, sweet Mrs. Parker. The flames were quickly extinguished.

My oldest son just reminded me not too long ago about a fire *he* started in *our* backyard. He was much older than I was when I got caught in this situation, so I must have "dropped the ball" with him somewhere along the way. But, it got taken care of *that* day!

I was just getting home from work. It was still light out and as I drove up into the driveway I could see black smoke coming up from behind the house. I hurried out of the car and into the backyard. There was this small fire, a pretty nice one, in the middle of the yard with four teen age boys standing around watching. This was in lush Mississippi with grass and trees, *and our house about 20 feet away and my large shed and garage about that same distance away! And, pine trees all the way around the yard!!*

Apparently, my son had looked out the back window and saw the dead stump of the tree we had cut down that the ants had taken over. So, he thought, "Let's pour gas on it and kill two birds with one stone (and maybe burn down the house and garage while we're at it!)!" Poof! All of it could have gone "up in smoke!"

"What are you guys doing?!" There were my three sons and a friend of theirs. When I realized who the guest was, I am told that I said something like, "What do you do, sit around the house and think, 'what dumb stuff can I do to impress Jack while he's here?!'"

Fortunately, no harm, no foul, and no out-of-control blaze. *I* was a little hot!

Then, there was the firecracker incident. Again, our sons were all teenagers at the time and they all had the male fascination with fireworks. I had let them buy some for the 4th and we had leftovers. We also were into firearms and a couple of the crackers we purchased were small targets about 2 inches square. They were *designed* to be mounted on a backboard or post out on a gun range and exploded by shooting them with a gun.

Well, our middle son got the bright (that may not be the right word for it) idea (this may not be the right word either) to take one of those TARGETS out to the gravel driveway WITH a hammer! Are you getting the picture, yet? This is our straight-A high school son! I didn't know what was going on until I looked out the kitchen window and saw him crouched down readying the hammer over his head. Then, it dawned on me. Before I could get out the door, "BLAM!" Gravel flew everywhere, my son staggered backward, and I was yelling at him scared, mad! PTL! He was not blinded, no lacerations or mangled limbs, but he did lose some hearing in his ears for a few days.

I could tell you about the five grown married men who wrapped sparkles with duck tape and made sparkler bombs on one 4th of July evening, but, instead, let's talk about some common sense advice that should be shared to keep tragedies and near tragedies from happening.

Maybe the answer is to sit down with your kids and explain the dangers of fire and give them some safety tips about fireworks. You can give them some examples of accidents that have happened, not necessarily telling them real names and faces, if you know what I mean. Go somewhere that you can have a safe controlled burn (Fire!), take some marshmallows, and, also, shoot off fireworks with them once a year. Just make sure that it is all legal and safe!

As men, we not only have this mesmerizing fetish for fire and all its related attractions, we also have a dull sense or awareness about where we have just taken our bodies with our footwear.

How many times have you come into the house, tromped through the kitchen or living room, only to hear your wife cry, "Look at the mess you're making on the floor (carpet)! You didn't even look at your shoes or wipe them before you stepped into the house!" Hopefully, you *did* do the clean up!

There are lots of hazards for your feet outside the walls of your home. Some of them can be prevented and some can't. There are water puddles in the street, oil spots on the driveway, mud holes in the field, and yes, doggy doo in the grass. Whether we see these hazards or not, we are responsible for where we have taken our footwear.

We owned a dog for several years, who was a good therapist for most of the boys. She loved to play with them, loved the attention, and it was the same for the boys. As she got older she started having more physical problems and one of them was allergies. I am pretty sure she was allergic to pollens and she must have known it too. It got to the point when the grass was growing during the spring and summer, she would not travel too far from the door to do her business when she was let outside, always in the backyard.

One day I was out on the front lawn in a serious conversation with two of my sons. Apparently, our dear house pet had snuck out the door with one of us. As I started to go back inside not far from the front steps, I stepped and slid in something. I picked up my foot only to find, you got it, doggy doo! Except, that's not what I called it in the heat of that moment. I told it like it was and later had to apologize to my sons, who thought the whole thing was hilarious. I *did* apologize for the slip of the tongue.

The easy cure for this whole thing would be to follow the Asian tradition of removing our shoes at the door. All of our children have adopted this method since they have gotten married, and for those with multiple children, it's the only way to go!

I can't tell you how many times I have swept the floor, scrubbed carpet stains and vacuumed because somebody couldn't remember to check their feet before they walked halfway *or all* the way through the house! I'm guilty too!

Don't follow the traditions of the plumber and the appliance repairman. I'm not stereotyping here. It happened to me just a couple of months ago. Our kitchen sink had a dripping faucet that I could not cure. So, I called a *professional* who was also a friend and former customer of mine. He came and fixed the faucet, but left me with a dirty floor and carpet. That should take away a little from him being called a professional, shouldn't it?

If you are not going to remember to check your shoes outside or leave them in "the mud room," if you have one, then the Asian way is a pretty good option. It might be the best practice. My only problem, personally, is that I have no natural padding left on my feet, especially the right one. I have to have "a little bit of soul, yeah, a little bit of soul" on my feet at all times. So, please forgive me if I don't remove my shoes when I come over. I'll bring my Crocs to change into.

By the way, the best and cheapest thing to clean most of those everyday carpet stains is good old-fashioned Windex with ammonia and a clean rag. I have been using that for 27 years.

Chapter 7

Home Improvements and Christmas Packing by Anti-Claus

As I have said, you can learn a lot from reading, *and* you can learn a lot from your own mistakes, if you want to. I also told you that reading has not always been easy for me. But, what many times has been an issue for me, and for others, has been the lack of reading. This lack is what gets me into trouble *a lot*!

I *do* think it's true about men not reading the instructions or not following the directions or not reading the map. This is *no* stereotype! I can't believe it's just me! Come on! How about the rest of you?! "Confession is good for the soul!"

I never took geometry or calculus in school, barely passed two years of algebra, probably should have failed it (some more of that "social promotion" stuff) but, I *can* do basic math; add, subtract, multiply, and divide. I have never taken a carpentry course, though, there was 8th grade woodshop. I never used a tool in that class, just sandpaper for the chest/trunk that was cut and nailed *for* me by the teacher. And, I have never read a book on carpentry or home improvements, although I think I've got one around here somewhere. So, what made me think I could *make* anything?! That's a good question! I just thought I could! Like The Little Engine That Could! I thought I could. I thought I could. I thought I could. I have two eyes, two hands and half a brain! Isn't that enough?

I was a pretty good bicycle repairman for the neighborhood as a teenager, and I did build and repair bikes for my sons when they were young. So, I did have that skill and really enjoyed it, too. Just one thing; be cautious about a neighbor kid giving you a 20 inch bike frame and building a cool new-to-you bike only to have a policeman drive up just as you have finished putting it together and tell you that it was from a stolen bike and you have to take it all apart again and give it to the officer. Find out where the frame came from first!

I have tried to do and have done many home and car repairs, because, number one, I want to save some money by doing it myself (You laugh). And, secondly, *because I like tools!* Hey, guys! We all like tools, especially *power tools*!

Let me share with you some of my "not so great" accomplishments with tools.

The Leaning Bookcase of CJ's

I remember the first thing that I actually made myself out of lumber. My wife and I were newly married and between her small library and the combination of our college textbooks, we ran out of shelf space. We needed another bookcase. No big deal! "I'll build one!" I must have had the wood precut at the lumber yard, because, at the time I didn't own much in the way of tools, just some hand wrenches and sockets from my bike repairing days. I hadn't inherited my first jigsaw and drill as yet.

How I got the bookcase assembled must have been pretty barbaric with only a hammer and nails. I did get it together, stained it, and even attached an eighth inch piece of masonite for the back. For some reason, though, it wanted to lean forward instead of setting up parallel with the wall. Again, "no big deal!" I just put some shims under the front and it sat up straight.

We hauled this homemade looking clunker of a bookcase around with us for six moves. During our most recent move, it was time to let it go. I don't remember if I let my sons tear it apart to start a *fire* or if we just gave it away with so much other stuff that we would not have room for. But, it's gone, and *no* great loss.

The Two Man Toolbox

By the time I attempted my next great project, I did have more tools, including a drill, a jigsaw and a circular saw. I needed something to carry them in because I had tried to start my own handyman and lawn care business. So, I built a carpenter's toolbox out of a bunch of scrap lumber I had collected from some construction sites.

I had seen my father-in-law's box that he had inherited from his father and I knew that one like it would be too small for what I needed. When I got mine put together and loaded with tools, it took two men to pick it up, and *I was the only man around*! I guess I had made a truck box instead of a one man carpenter's box. After time it became the catch-all for leftover nails, screws and chunks of wire, plastic plumbing pipe, and, you name it.

Let me give you a hint here. You don't need 2by lumber to make a toolbox. Half inch plywood is sufficient. I ended up hauling this loaded with tools from CO to MS. But, also, it was left behind during our last move. I didn't have a place for it and couldn't pick it up anyway!

The Wayward Drill

If you own a vehicle or two, they need repairs from time to time. No kidding! Twenty or thirty years ago, the average guy with some halfway decent hand tools could do some minor repairs. I have done my share and many of them were successful, and some not. The one that my family remembers most vividly, because, to them it was quite humorous, required me using my drill to reattach a door latch on our minivan.
Let me see if I can describe this event and see if *you* think it's *so* funny.

Apparently, due to wear and vibration, both screws had worked loose from the latch on the front passenger's door. All I needed to do was drill the holes a little bigger and put in two pop rivets. Pretty smart, I thought. Pop rivets weren't going anywhere!

For some reason, in the process of putting pressure on the drill, it shifted, slipped or kicked back away from the door and headed right for my ribcage and went into my polo shirt. At this point, I let off the trigger and realized I was in a dilemma. I stood up holding on to the drill with one hand, unplugged it from the carport receptacle with the other hand, and walked into the house.

Once inside, I called to my family for someone to come, "Help me!" All they could do was stand there and laugh at me and try, through their laughter, to ask how I had gotten into this predicament. My shirt was so baggy that before my senses told me to let off the trigger, the drill bit had wound up into the side of my shirt just below my right armpit. My skin had been saved, but my wife and son had to work to get the bit out of the twisted up shirt. Unbelievably, it only had a small hole in it. I whip stitched it and still have that shirt to this day (one of my daughters-in-law thinks I should get rid of it).

Perhaps the sad thing about car repairs for me is that I took auto mechanics all through high school. I thought I wanted to have my own repair shop. Here again, it would have helped if I had read the instructions, "the textbook" during year one of the class. I had to have read *some* of it in order to answer the questions for each chapter. Once again, this was in a school system that pretty much left students on their own. And, in this case, this is just what the teacher did with this class. About a dozen 15 and 16 year old boys were left alone during most of the one hour period of our sophomore year and also for the three hour periods in our junior and senior years. What's more, when the teacher *was* present for class and a student needed some help with a repair, instead of giving some instruction or assistance, he just got under the car and did it himself. How was he teaching anything? Who was *learning* anything?

Does this sound like a bunch of "sour grapes" on my part? I do accept some of the blame for not being more disciplined and mature. I wasn't. But, I thought the whole point of school was for teaching and instructing students! Wah! Wah! Wah! Pass the cheese and make it Swiss, please!

It was probably after my fiasco with the drill and van door that I started getting all the comic birthday and Father's Day cards from my sons. I have seven of them that I could find. There may have been more, but here are some lines from them;

Happy Father's Day to the guy who taught me everything I need to know about Hand Tools. Which is: Hand the tools to you and step back!

Here's a little something for the "Do-It-Yourself Dad" who's so handy around the house... (open the card and you see) a band aid!

Dad, when they made you, they broke the mold…and you fixed it!! (only now it won't close right, and it sort of veers off to the left…) Try not to think about it and have a Happy Birthday!

Happy Father's day to the man who taught me the difference between a ball-peen and a claw hammer… and what to say when I hit my thumb! "Dag nab it!"

Wishing an unforgettable man…a Father's Day to remember. "Absolutely 'unforgettable'… like I'll never forget that time you came into the house with a drill hanging from your shirt! I love you dad!"

Let's return to "the adventures of home improvements", a much funnier *and* more creative subject coming from a self-taught, not-so-handyman.

The Stoop *Under* Stoop Cover

I wrote earlier about how to help keep the floors clean at home. One thing I did at our house was to build a cover or roof over the back stoop or *porch*, for those who may not be acquainted with the other name.

Once again, I was able to salvage free materials from the place that I worked. The company was adding on to the building and they had to remove a nice sized aluminum dock cover. I only needed to take part of the scrap and was given permission to do so. If I do say so myself, I was able to put together a nice sturdy cover. Now all I needed were two 4x4x10 foot cedar posts for standards. I did all the figuring in my mind and got to work. Fortunately, I already had a posthole digger from fencing jobs I did a few years earlier. Now there's a job I really enjoyed and learned a lot from… building fence. Maybe that should be the next story. I was trying to do this chapter in chronological order. Oh Well! This isn't an autobiography, but close! Let me get back to the porch cover.

I dug the holes and set the posts about two feet deep. Then, I held the cover up against the house and on to the posts, measured how much of an angle was needed for run- off, and how much post needed to be cut from the tops.

Maybe that's not how I did it. I'm confused, and that is actually the state of mind I was in that day, "a confused state of mind." I think I forgot how far down the posts were set, so I cut one foot off the top of them, only to discover, once I held the cover up, that my six foot tall person had to duck to get under it to step up the steps, a dead give-away that I had "screwed *up!!*"

I didn't need to cut 12 inches off, only *two* inches! What could I do? Well, there was only one thing that I *could* do. I had to take the one foot chunks and screw them back on to the tops of the posts! Good thing this was on the *back* stoop! The only ones who were going to see it were my family and a couple of good friends. They were all amused and a little concerned that I had miscalculated, *again*.

The Winter of Fence

I did mention fence building. Let's go back about 16 years. I had quit a teaching position at a school in California, because I felt like I didn't know what I was doing, and that I was not able to help those students as much as they needed it. Boy, did a *bunch* of them need *a lot* of help!

We packed up in early November of 1979 and moved to Colorado with no job to go to and moved in next door to my wife's family. They had a cute little one bedroom, one bath house that the four of us crowded into.

In time, I had worked a few one day jobs that were assigned by the local temp agency. By early Spring in March of 1980, I still had not found steady work. That's when my caring in-laws, and I *mean* that in the truest and most sincere way, came up with a job for me.

They lived on the north end outside of a small town on two acres of prairie on a hill overlooking some of the most beautiful mountain country in Colorado. I believe it was my mother-in-law who really came up with the idea, and that idea was to have me fence in their property. They had lived there for almost twenty years without fence, but they knew I needed something to do and besides, it would probably increase their property value if they were ever to sell. And, years later, they did, and it did!

So, in the dead of winter, it's still very *much* winter in the foothills of the Rockies in March, with no previous experience at fence building or at operating a tractor with a frontend loader and backhoe, I jumped in. Thankfully, there was a good friend of the family who lived a few miles north who had plenty of hours under his belt with tractors and fence. He had to end up giving me some much needed advice in why my first section of fence was sagging, how to build cedar post centers and corners for stability, and how to drive and pull up tee posts with a driver and high man jack.

If you know anything about Colorado winters you know that it can snow 6 inches one day and the next day be sunny and 70 degrees, and melt it all away. This is exactly the kind of weather I was working in. Overalls, long johns, gloves, and a hooded coat were my complete attire for two months or so. There were days that were sunny and beautiful and I was working in my shirt sleeves.

Oh yes! I also learned how to use an eight foot steel bar to break through roots and shale rock in order to get some post holes deep enough to set the cedars.

There were a few days that were pretty tough and some that I could not even work. It was hard to put up fence when it was snowing "to beat the band," or on those two occasions when I got the tractor stuck due to all the snow melting and making that prairie dust and shale turn into rocky mud. Talk about "a hard day's night and I've been working like a dog." And feeling like a wet noodle, but it was a good wet noodle feeling. I was enjoying this job. I was learning stuff, stuff that I don't think I could have learned from a book. There are some jobs that the best way to learn them is by doing! This was certainly one of them.

Now that I think about it, that has been true for most of the jobs I've worked. They call it "on-the-job-training." I sat down one day not too long ago and tried to remember all of the jobs that I have had in the last 45 years. At 60 years of age, I have worked at least 34 different jobs. That's an average of 1.76 years per job. The longest I have stayed with any one company is five and a half years. This gives you more of an idea of what my wife has had to put up with. Job hopping is not the way I planned my work experience, my career to go. If I could have a "do over," I would hope that I would do differently.

Since I knew that I was not a real auto mechanic after graduating from high school, I went to Bible College, got degrees in pastoral theology and music, and pastored one church for two and a half years. I was sure that this was what I would be doing for the rest of my life. Wrong again?

My advice here would be "don't do as I have done," *do better!* Find a vocation, a job, a career in a field that you have talents and ability and that you at least halfway enjoy. If it's honest, profitable, secure, and a service to others, stick with it!! This will go a long way in providing stability and security for you and your family. It may give you enough material to write your own book someday.

The Recliner Attack

There was one time that I was attempting to fix something and didn't get any further along than trying to inspect the problem when sudden chaos broke out. We owned this old, worn, stained, getting ugly, rust colored upholstered chair that was in the family room. The dog and I had pretty much taken over ownership of this only recliner in the house.

For some reason the handle to raise the foot rest was stuck. It would not come up! So, while I was in my underwear, why just my underwear, I don't remember, with the whole family in the room, I turned the chair on its side to get a look at the situation. With *no* tool in my hand, which was probably a *good* thing in hind sight, I knelt down beside the chair, grabbed the foot rest handle (lever), and looked under it. I guess I was trying to move the lever and see why it was not releasing, when, "Smack!" Something, to this day I don't know what, smacked me in my forehead right below the hairline. It felt like somebody hit me with a pick hammer! I verbalized some kind of noise that indicated pain, while my whole body flew off the floor and landed about six feet away from the chair. I ended up in the fetal position on the carpet, moaning in agony.

My wife and three sons did not know what in the world had happened. I think they were all watching TV, and they all just sat in silence, shock and wonder. After a few seconds, when the pain had subsided and I showed no signs of a cracked skull or profuse bleeding, and my family figured that I was going to live, the laughter started. "What was that all about? What happened? Are you alright? That was hilarious!! Did you see that? He just flew back and hit the floor!!"

What compassion! Because I was not bleeding much and did not have another new hole in my head, they felt free to let out the emotion that turned from concern and wonder to a great opportunity for "a cheerful heart that is good medicine." I guess it was pretty funny seeing their gangly husband/dad in his underwear flying across the room and lying all curled up on the floor. I was attempting a repair, got hurt and didn't even have a tool in my hand!! I don't even remember if the chair ever got fixed. It must be that smack in the head.

Are you seeing any other lessons that you can take away from all this? Read a how-to book, the textbook, or the instruction manual, whichever the case may be! If you like tools and want to use them safely, take a course or find someone who knows how to use them and teach you! What's the computer for that you're holding in your hand or sitting in front of? GOOGLE it! "How to…," whatever you need to do.

If you can't do it right and carefully, save yourself the pain, humiliation and embarrassment, *Hire a professional*! But, maybe I'm all wet and don't know what I'm talking about. In that case, it may be time for Ed's Prayer;

Mr. D., I've got a prayer for you. I want you to say it every night. "Dear Lord, I love you. Thank You for this day and for loving me. But, please help me to keep my mouth shut when I don't know what I'm talkin' about! In Jesus Name, amen!"

This is a real, spontaneous prayer that was offered in my living room with my sons present by a friend who was then college age. I was giving him some advice which must have been unsolicited and must have been somewhat skewed. Once again, there was raucous laughter from the reciting of this prayer.

I do have one suggestion about a good tool, if you are in the market for one. If you like demolition projects, because, like me, you can't make a straight cut even with a caulk line, you've got to get yourself a reciprocating saw! Oh man, what a tool!! Like "cutting hot butter," wood or metal.

One last story and I'll wrap up this crazy thing. As I mentioned in the acknowledgments, my three sons keep feeding me ammo that is helping fill these pages, and this last Christmas is material that just can't go to waste.

The Wrath of Anti-Claus

This story really starts back in the 1940's or so, when my mother was a little girl. Between my mother and her mom, grandmother K., there were several quilts and afghans that had been made of different styles, colors and sizes. What grandma had collected when she died was passed on to my mother. Mom wanted to give each of her grandchildren the blessing of inheriting some of this useful nostalgic memorabilia. Our sons were given the opportunity to choose a quilt and an afghan, which they all did.

These pieces of family history were boxed up and transported from Colorado to Mississippi and stored with us for years. Before we knew it the boys had grown and gone, but their precious treasures remained with mom and dad. There were times these could have been taken by them or delivered to them, but we just forgot. I did remember on one flight back to Colorado a few years ago, where two of our sons now live, to carry one set in my luggage.

This last Christmas I remembered again, and was determined to get these other two sets out of our attic and into the boy's attics, closets, or wherever they were going to end up in *their* houses!

My wife and I were driving to OK where the oldest lived, giving him his set, then he and his family would drive to Colorado and deliver the last set. My wife and I flew from OK to Denver and the whole family was to meet north of Denver for Christmas week.

Along with the quilts and afghans were all of the Christmas gifts from us to our children, grandchildren and daughters-in-law that my wife had spent all day one Saturday so beautifully wrapping in her organized and creative way. The wife and I couldn't have all of these on the plane, so these gifts were packed into two large boxes which were also given to the OK clan to transport. I asked that they *be sure* and carry them in the van to protect them from the weather and *not* be tied on the metal carrier attached to the back bumper. I believe I even used the word "please!" These were *the gifts* for 13 family members for Christmas!

This is becoming kind of a lengthy scenario, but I'll try "to make a long story short" by "cutting to the chase." Of course, 10 of us were in Colorado before the OK group even left to head that way. They took the southern route driving through Texas and then into NM to try and avoid bad weather. This had them traveling about straight west for most of the day battling a strong cross wind, then turning north. Somewhere in NM, my son and his wife started smelling something strange and pungent. There happened to be a gas station just up ahead, so they pulled into the parking area beside it to check their load. As our son looked at the carrier loaded down with boxes and plastic totes, he noticed one tote was smoking and had a melted hole in the bottom corner of it. He quickly untied the tote, dragged it away from the van and opened it. This caused it to burst into flames from the supply of oxygen that immediately flowed in.

After getting help from the station attendant with two fire extinguishers and the fire department watching the whole thing from a distance, the tote fire was put out. This was the same son who years earlier thought it was a cool idea to douse gas on a dead tree stump to fry the ants. This was one fire he did *not* enjoy!

Guess what was in those totes that were tied on the *back* on the carrier *on the outside* of the van?! You guessed it half right! Some of the Christmas gifts *and* the one last set of cherished bed covers were packed together in one tote.

What caused the fire? Well, apparently, once they had turned north on their trip that day, the wind became a head wind and was blowing the hot exhaust right back on those totes with about 400 degree heat. 400 degrees will burn a lot of different materials and it had *plenty* of materials; cloth, paper, ribbons and bows, plastic, and it burned that day.

Most of the gifts were saved, though some were charred and all had the worst odor I have ever smelled in my life! The pungent odor was the combination of smoldering cloth, melted plastic, fire extinguishers, and carbon monoxide exhaust.

The sad, but humorous thing about all of this is what *didn't* survive the flaming smelly ordeal. The afghan and quilt were the fire starter. They were the items that were on the bottom of the tote and smoldered and burst into flames once oxygen was let in. But, they actually kept the gift boxes from catching fire right away. The carefully boxed and stored family heirlooms were sacrificed to save the Christmas packages. These old antiques that had been safe and sound for years as they were stored in closets and attics gave themselves for the new tokens of love which will live for years to come. If I had just left them in the attic they would still be with us today. Sounds pretty dramatic, huh?

Because of this ordeal, our son has been dubbed "The Anti-Claus" who almost burned up Christmas of 2014.

The moral of this story is, be sure to carry a fire extinguisher with you when you are packed up for a road trip, and don't have flammable items *on the outside* on the back of your vehicle close to the tail pipe that puts out 400 degrees of exhaust heat. Sounds pretty sensible, *doesn't it*?!

Chapter 8

Ball Games, Cross-Country and Mealtime

I love professional football. Well, I like it *a lot*. I have watched all of the world championship games for the last thirty years or more, and have seen some great ones. Who can forget Denver's back-to-back wins? John finally won! And then, the next year Kurt took St Louis to a 13 and 3 season and on to championship #34 (which is easier for me to read than XXXIV. I can read Roman numerals to about XXXIX. And, no, I haven't learned the metric system either! Hope I never have to). What a ride 1999 was for St Louis! Then there was Eli against Tom in #42. Loved it! But, probably my favorite game was the rematch of those two in #46. Keeping New England from scoring in the 1st and 4th quarters and winning 21 to 17, that was great!

Something happened when we moved to Mississippi 27 years ago. I had *heard* of college football, but had never watched any. College football, humph! Bunch of amateurs!

It seemed that everybody in the South was *crazy* about college ball of all sorts! So, I tried watching some of their football games. Still didn't get into it much. Then we moved to north MS, lived in an apartment for seven months, didn't know anybody, had not found a church yet, and I was working nights part time. There wasn't much for me to do during the day and I felt like a zombie from working all night, so I turned on the TV one Saturday afternoon in September of 2003 (pronounced "twenty-03", this year being "twenty-fifteen) and caught the second half of Florida vs. Miami. By the third quarter Florida had Miami 35 to 0. Miami's quarterback was a former quarterback of Florida and something must of happened during halftime or just clicked for him in that 3rd quarter, because after it was all said and done, Miami came back to beat Florida 38 to 35. Thirty-eight unanswered points! Now *that* was a game! I started getting interested in those amateurs by that time. Hope I haven't bored you with my football trivia.

As I write this, another season of pro and college football is over with the world championship game less than two weeks away. Number 49 (or XLIX. I had to flip over to nfl.com to see how to type it in Roman numerals)! It's been great to be involved this year by getting chores done Saturday morning and church Sunday morning, then grab some lunch, sit down in the old loveseat or recliner, and cheer on my favorite teams from noon to after nine at night. I used to loathe all of the TV commercials, especially the beer ads. Those have always seemed to be out of place with sports to me. I know that they sell the stuff at stadiums and that probably lots of fans drink it at home during the games, so why advertise it so cotton pickin' much?! It's not like nobody is buying the stuff! Just keep the cameras on the field and the stands!!

As I was saying, I used to loathe most of the ads. But now I need them to give me breaks to get off my duff and stretch my legs and keep the sciatica from kicking in.

The great thing about televised sports of *any* kind is that you don't have to go anywhere, fight the crowds or wonder where and when you are going to eat your next meal. After paying over a hundred dollars for a ticket, if you are able to get to a pro game, who can afford to buy stadium food! And, who wants to walk a mile to go to the restroom after downing that stupid 32 ounce soda?! You can still be involved with sports by rooting for the team, yelling at the refs, players and coaches, and learning more about the sport with each passing game, *right in your own home*!

This is all much more difficult when it's your children who are engaged in elementary, middle and high school sports. Then you have to pack up the car, drive to the particular venue, fight the crowds, endure the weather, and make some kind of plans on occasion as to how to you are going to fill your stomach if a game is scheduled around an important mealtime. You can pack a meal, but it ain't gonna be *no picnic*!

Can you imagine what it was like with thirteen boys at the children's home when most of them thought that they had to play sports?! It was hectic enough with four or five playing baseball trying to get them on the same teams, so that practices and games could be at the same time and place. Fortunately, with elementary kids, all their games were at the multiplex ball park right in town.

How about soccer? First of all, I might have to agree with the rest of the world that a better name for this game *is* football. You do use only your feet to play the sport. But, then, what about American football? It gets kind of confusing. Ninety-five percent of the time in American football you use your hands to hike, pass, catch, and hold the ball while running for a *"touchdown!"* The only time anybody uses their feet is for punts, kick offs and field goals. Well, there are a couple of pro players who use their feet for other things on the field like stomping on an opponent's head or ankle. I'm not going to mention any names, but there is one pro defensive player who used to be on a Michigan team, but is now with a Miami team, whose last name sounds just like what someone may do with his pants in a courtroom someday. Compendia, amigos?

Getting back to the name of the sport, I guess you could call American football *tackle ball*, because that is what every player on the defense is trying to do to the guy carrying the ball! Should I start a petition?

Our middle son joined up with the high school soccer team and did pretty well, at least that is what he and his mother told me. They play this sport in the dead of winter! Why do they have to play in the cold and the wind and the rain and the slop?! I guess they have to wait until football season is over, so that any of those players that want to join can get on the team.

I can only remember going to one game that was played in town. I suppose that I'm somewhat of a wimp, but *you* don't have to be. Just do what I should have done and put on your big boy pants, raincoat and goulashes, and go to the games!

Cross-country meets are *another* animal. The name pretty much says it all. If you have a child that likes to run and joins this sport, plan on going *cross-country*! These were all miles away from home. The away games were *away*, one to three hours from where we lived. Whoever planned these meets didn't seem to give a hoot about parent's sanity or the participant's safety. All of those long distant drives in the dark late at night. As I remember, most of these meets were during the week, not on weekends.

There was a lot of travel which made for some late nights. Mama felt the need to support her son who was doing cross-country and went to most, if not to all of the meets. Daddy was too tired after a long day of work and stayed home with the other two boys. At least, I think that was my excuse. Like I said, I'm a wimp! I don't like to drive at night, I don't like to be out in inclement weather, and after going through all of that, I don't like to see my boy lose. I did make it to two or three of the meets, I'm sure due to some strong persuasion and because I *did* want my son to know that I cared about what he was doing.

Here's another time in my life I wish I could have a "do over." I would make it to more meets and ball games.

Just a couple words of advice on all this; number one, don't drive yourself insane by over-commitment. Help your children understand that there is a reasonable amount of things that they can be involved in. Find a balance for *everybody's* sake. Plan meals around them if you have to. Make the meals easy, but as healthy as you can. We all know what ball park food is like, and haven't we all had enough of *Mickey D's*?! And, when you do go to your kids' sporting events, don't be one of those loud, rude, angry, and embarrassing parents that makes a big scene when things don't go well for their poor little Johnny or Jane. It's only a game, *for cryin' out loud*!!

Hey! If this all comes too late for you and you know that you messed up, didn't get involved enough, and they're all grown up and gone now, just grab a sandwich, a bag of chips and have a seat. The ball game's about to start!

Chapter 9

Church Going, Rubber Bands and Candy Wrappers

Congratulations to those of you who have gotten this far in the book! I hope that you have had a few chuckles along the way and have discovered some areas in your life that you can improve upon.

Now here's a subject that I could have written this whole book on. I have plenty of experience on this matter, all the "do's and don'ts", especially the don'ts. After all, I have been in church from the first Sunday that my mother took me after my birth until now, and I'm 61 years old. Of course, I have missed Sundays due to sickness and travel. Having grown up in churches of the independent, strict sort with a legalistic slant, I can definitely tell you about the "don'ts" to be a good little rules keeper. Here's the short list:

-don't drink alcoholic beverages

-don't cuss

-don't dance

-don't smoke or chew tobacco

-don't wear make-up

-don't wear tight pants

-don't wear short skirts

-don't smile until Jesus comes!

Don't get me wrong. I am so thankful that Mom and Dad took me to church every Sunday morning, Sunday evening, Wednesday evening, and any other time there was a meeting going on. I'm sure it spared me from getting into more trouble than I already got into!

After growing up and going to college, I married a woman who experienced a similar church life, and then, the very same Bible college atmosphere (where we met and fell in love) and teaching that I did. Though I do not agree with some of the traditions and attitudes that we were taught or caught in those younger years, I do believe in the truth from the Scriptures that were revealed to me, and now, strive to live out daily.

Since those formative years I have learned that there are many more "do's" than "don'ts." Once again, here's a short list:

-do love God with your whole being

-do love others as yourself "especially those of the household of faith"

-do read your Bible as often as possible

-do pray every day

-do respect earthly authorities which God has ordained

-do be thankful for everything

-do love your children enough to teach them right from wrong

-do try and remember to smile and "rejoice always!"

Even though I was a pretty active child and had trouble sitting still in school, I did much better in church. This was probably due to the fact that Mom and Dad were *with me* in church. Also, I liked being around people, liked singing, and if it wasn't singing time, I learned to draw pictures of men and race cars. I learned the style of drawing from the church organist who was a good family friend and whom I was allowed to sit with *on the front row* on the right side of the sanctuary. But, you can bet that once the service was over and I was able to get through the crowd to the front door, I was outside running and yelling my silly head off, and probably chasing somebody!

My advice to you, if you have a child or children who may be on the border of ADHA, or just have the little kid normality of "ants in their pants", be sure and sing with them during hymn time and pack a bag for church with some pencils and paper to help keep them from interrupting the pastor and embarrassing you during the sermon. Who knows, they may even start taking notes (or more like writing notes and passing them to their friend in the next row)!

The Rubber Band Surprise

By the time it was my turn to experience what it was like to get a family to church and keep them in line, we had three sons ages 1, 3, and 5, and I was the pastor! We were pastoring a small church in my home town and my wife was the pianist. One Sunday morning the three boys (about 2 1/2, 4 1/2 and 6 1/2 at the time), were sitting in the front pew (a pew is a long wooden bench, in case you thought it was something else) just about three feet away from where my wife was seated at the piano. Now, I'm not sure what was going on at the moment, but I was on the platform and all of a sudden I heard, *everyone* heard my youngest son start howling and crying as if he had just been slapped on his bare back side by one of his parents.

Fortunately, his back side *was not* bare and his mama sprang from the piano to take him out of the sanctuary and figure out what had just happened. I found out after the service what provoked such an outburst and tears. Somehow, he, the 2 1/2 year old, had ended up with a rubber band and had it on two fingers on one hand. He then proceeded to pulled it back away from his face with the other hand, let go, and popped himself right in the kisser. You know *that* hurt! You've been snapped by a rubber band by someone before, either in the arm or leg, and know how much it can sting. Just imagine getting popped in the face! And doing it to yourself! To add insult to injury, his brothers, sitting next to him, saw what was going on, watched the whole thing, and couldn't help laughing. We made sure from then on that rubber bands never made it to their seats in church. Make sure that your kid's church pack doesn't include any lethal weapons.

A Sweet For The Sweets?

There are some other methods of keeping kids still during church, two of which I will mention briefly. First, there is the threat of discipline during and/or after church service for any misbehavior. This works with the compliant child, but for the others who have a hard time trying not to be a kid in church, it can be more difficult. I wonder how much they are really able to pay attention to the sermon and if they are worrying about whether they are going to receive some kind of punishment soon after the closing prayer.

The other is the-bag-of-candy-in-the-wife's-purse method. It's called bribery! "If you can be a good boy/girl during church, I'll give you some candy!"

One caution; be sure the candy is out of the cellophane wrap which can be heard from the pulpit to the foyer just when you decide little Johnnie or Jane needs it to help keep his/her sweet mouth quiet. Put the candy in a sandwich bag. And only carry sour lemon drops, so the child will be occupied with sucking instead of talking and won't be able to whistle either.

Here is something that you need to make a routine. Do everything you can to avoid the Sunday-morning-rush-before-we're-late-for-church frenzy. On Saturday evening polish the church shoes, iron the shirts/dresses, have church clothes laundered, make sure the car has enough gas, and bathe/shower the children. What *else* is there to do on Saturday night?

As if having three sons of our own was not enough for us to try and figure how to raise, we became houseparents at the children's home to ten more! I didn't have a job at the time and the Lord opened up this one. Besides, our boys thought it would be cool to have ten more brothers! Our sons were 6, 8, and 10 at the time. My wife and I figured that we had ten years of experience under our belts and had done pretty well. We could do this!

If you haven't gained some common sense by then, or just having your own family wasn't enough reason for you to strive for maturity, it's time to "sink or swim," "grow up or shut up" with thirteen boys ages 5 to 12 years old! These boys know if you are for real or not. From the backgrounds that they have come out of, they have been around the blocks that you didn't even know existed. In this situation you can grow up yourself in a hurry if you want to. You need to!

Another thing, if you haven't learned the need for prayer before this, it is a good time to learn and start doing a lot of it! A time like this should bring you to your knees to seek Divine guidance. If it doesn't, you must be one of the smartest people in the world, or not.

Much to our relief, the first boys we came to parent at the children's home knew how to behave in church. It was those new ones who came along that caused me to dig deep for answers. God was good! I made my share of mistakes, but we ran the cottage of elementary boys with consistency and a routine that made things operate pretty smoothly. And, I hope that most of those boys learned that there is a God Who loves them, *and* realized the importance of taking a shower more than once a week.

I have just one more thing to mention about church attendance. If you don't want to give your wife the feeling of insecurity and prove to her your immaturity, *don't* church hop! Find a church that teaches the truth and has some good programs for your whole family. Put away some of your preferences about things that do not go against the important doctrines of Scripture. Make church a stable, peaceful, spiritually profitable priority for your family!

Whew! I think it's time for a lemon drop!

Conclusion

Now that I have led you on for these nine brief chapters, I need to tell you this, there is really no such thing as "common sense." I did just read the second section of Dr. Ben Carson's book "One Nation" and he says this about common sense on page 139;

> Wisdom is essentially the same thing as common sense, the slight difference is that common sense provides the ability to react appropriately, while wisdom is frequently more proactive and additionally encourages the shaping of the environment.

I disagree with him, somewhat, on this point. Common sense is actually wisdom in laymen's terms. No one is naturally endowed with it! Dr. Carson does go on to say that "wisdom is the most important commodity for anyone who is planning to be successful in any endeavor." We agree *fully* on this point.

Please, don't feel like I have just dragged you along on a false premise. Would you really have read this if the title was something like "Grow Up! Knucklehead! Just Grow Up!"? Well, maybe you would have. That is precisely what this is all about. So, grow up (mature)! Get smart (wisdom)! Be the mature, balanced adult that you are supposed to be!

This book doesn't have a lot of answers. It's not "a silver bullet." *I'm* still very much "a piece of work" in progress. I just want to pass on the little that I'm learning and hope it helps somebody else. It all comes down to learning from those around you and listening to them, by watching them, and reading their writings and experiences, their sharing of knowledge.

The number one source for maturity and wisdom is the Bible. Read it! Study it and pray for God's guidance with thanksgiving. The wisest man who ever lived, outside of Jesus Christ Himself, said that the most important thing to have in life is wisdom, "common sense!" Hear some of King Solomon's words of wisdom;

> Getting wisdom is the most important thing you can do! And whatever else you do, get good judgment. If you prize wisdom, she will exalt you. Embrace her and she will honor you. She will place a lovely wreath on your head; she will present you with a beautiful crown.
> My child, listen to me and do as I say, and you will have a long, good life. I will teach you wisdom's ways and lead you in straight paths. If you live a life guided by wisdom, you won't limp or stumble as you run. Carry out my instructions; don't forsake them. Guard them, for they will lead you to a fulfilled life. (Proverbs 4: 7-13).

By the way, this "getting of wisdom" is not a one-time thing. It's daily! And, too, along with getting the wisdom that you need comes *change*. You have to be willing to change. If you are not changing, growing, maturing, you are dying. So, be alive, grow!

March on!

Printed in the United States
By Bookmasters